CLASSIC FANTASY

EXPERT SET

By

Rodney Leary

Cover by Dan MacKinnon

Interior Art by Eric Lofgren, Dan MacKinnon
& William McAusland

Classic Fantasy © 2016 by The Design Mechanism
Mythras is a Trademark of The Design Mechanism.
Interior artwork © 2016 Eric Lofgren, used with permission. All rights reserved.

All rights reserved. This edition of Classic Fantasy Expert Set is copyright © 2016.
This book may not be reproduced in whole or in part by any means without permission from The Design Mechanism, except as quoted for purposes of illustration, discussion and game play. Reproduction of the material in this book for the purposes of personal or corporate profit, by photographic, electronic, or other methods of retrieval is strictly prohibited.

Welcome...

To the Classic Fantasy *Expert Set*, a sampler for the forthcoming *Unearthed Companion*. The Expert Set is a supplement featuring a sample of higher rank spells, as well as several options and official changes to the Classic Fantasy rules. Finally, as a special bonus, a powerful monster of classic gaming has been included to serves as a terrifying opponent for high level play.

What's Included?

Rules Additions (Page 3)
Since Classic Fantasy's release, many awesome ideas and suggestions have been provided by the community. This chapter compiles a number of them in one convenient location, as well as including several that cut from the core book due to space restrictions.

Arcane and Divine Spells (Pages 7 & 13)
These chapters contain powerful Arcane and Divine spells of Ranks 4 and 5, and includes magics that can alter the very fabric of reality. They can strike an opponent dead with a single word; collapse castle walls with mighty quakes; gate in powerful entities from the outer planes; raise the dead, and even allow the caster and her allies to travel the vary planes of existence.

The Mind Slayer & Psychic Powers (Pages 25 & 26)
The infamous mind slayer is detailed for Classic Fantasy, alongside rules for psionic powers.

Updated Encounter & Magic Tables (Pages 29-32)
As a final bonus, the Wandering monster tables have been expanded to include creatures typically found on dungeon levels six and seven, home to the newly added Mind Slayer. Master Spell Tables are included for spells added in this document, and a new character sheet has been included based on that found in Mythras, and upgraded for Classic Fantasy use.

Updated Character Sheet
And finally, a revised character sheet for Classic Fantasy characters.

Rules Additions

Classic Fantasy has lots of moving parts, and as such, some things that should have been noticed were not. Therefore, this chapter collects the most important oversights together. This chapter also collects some of the better ideas that have been presented by the community since Classic Fantasy's release, and includes a few changes to address some perceived balance issues. They can be incorporated into your campaign, or ignored, as you wish.

Characters

Dice Roll Method
Change to read: "Roll one extra die and drop the lowest result, as indicated for STR, CON, SIZ, DEX, INT, POW, and CHA as detailed in the Racial Stat Blocks in Chapter 2".

Passion Changes
In Classic Fantasy, Lawful and Chaotic are Traits belonging to the Moral Philosophies of Good and Evil respectively. However, in many level-based games, Lawful and Chaotic are independent of the morality of the character, and can be applied to Good, Neutral, or Evil in equal measure. If this option is used, add Chaotic and Lawful to each of the Moral Philosophies on page 30 of Classic Fantasy, allowing characters of Good (Chaotic), Evil (Lawful), and Neutral (Lawful or Chaotic) to be created.

Character Class Changes
As the heart and soul of Classic Fantasy, character classes are one of its most important aspects. The following changes and additions both fix an omission or two, and offer several balance changes.

Prerequisite Skills
Each class has five Prerequisite skills that are used for advancement. However, many players have pointed out that these five skills do not leave much room for diversity, with each member of a particular class needing the same skills. This option assumes the prerequisite skills noted in Classic Fantasy represent an average member of the class, and goes on to give each class seven or eight skills, from which they choose the five that will define their development. Skills marked with an asterix represent those needed for spell casting or other supernatural abilities, and are important for the class in question. In the case of the paladin and ranger, these skills will still need to be taken at some point if they intend to be able to cast spells at Rank 3, and the skill will still need to be at 50% or higher to do so. However, it is no longer required for them to be taken during character creation.

Bard (Arcane)
Arcane Casting*, Arcane Knowledge*, Athletics, Influence, Lore (any), Musicianship, Seduction, Sing

Bard (Druidic)
Athletics, Channel*, Influence, Lore (any), Musicianship, Piety (Nature Deity)*, Sing, Survival

Berserker
Athletics, Brawn, Combat Style (Berserker), Endurance, Evade, Unarmed, Survival

Cavalier
Bureaucracy, Combat Style (Cavalier), Courtesy, Endurance, Influence, Ride, Willpower

Cleric
Channel*, Combat Style (Cleric), First Aid, Influence, Insight, Piety (Specific Deity)*, Willpower

Druid
Channel*, First Aid, Locale, Perception, Piety (Nature Deity)*, Survival, Willpower

Fighter
Brawn, Combat Style (Fighter), Craft (any weapon or armour related), Endurance, Evade, Lore (Strategy and Tactics), Unarmed

Magic-user
Arcane Casting*, Arcane Knowledge*, Influence, Insight, Lore (any), Perception, Willpower

Monk
Acrobatics, Athletics, Combat Style (Monk), Evade, Meditation*, Mysticism*, Unarmed, Willpower

Paladin
Channel*, Combat Style (Paladin), Courtesy, Influence, Insight, Piety (Nimue)*, Ride, Willpower

Ranger
Athletics, Channel*, Combat Style (Ranger), Endurance, Perception, Piety (Specific Nature Deity)*, Stealth, Survival

Thief
Athletics, Combat Style (Thief), Deceit, Evade, Slight, Stealth, Streetwise

Thief-Acrobat
Acrobatics, Athletics, Combat Style (Thief), Deceit, Evade, Perception, Stealth, Streetwise

Combat Proficiency
Classes with this talent, specifically the Berserker, Cavalier, Fighter, Monk, Paladin, and Ranger, should apply the +5% bonus to Unarmed in addition to their Combat Style. This was intended all along but did not actually state it explicitly. Note also that the Cavalier write-up incorrectly refers to this ability as Weapon Proficiency.

Berserker Changes
As stated in CLASSIC FANTASY, when raging, the berserker's Damage Modifier is increased 1 step for every 2 ranks. Remember that unless noted otherwise, all fractions round up, so the bonus is gained at ranks 1, 3, and 5.

The following changes to the Berserker class allow for the character to continue gaining abilities after Rank 1. These rules should be considered as official.

At Rank 1, the berserker gains the following additional abilities:

Resilient: Berserkers are incredibly resilient to the effects of wounds. Their Hit Points are calculated using STR+CON+SIZ.

Agile: The berserker gains superb reflexes. When calculating Initiative the character adds one tenth of his or her Athletics skill to the Initiative 1d10 roll. For example, a berserker with Athletics 60% would calculate Initiative on the Initiative base, +1d10+6.

Upon Reaching Rank 2, an expenditure of 2 Experience Rolls and 1 month of training allows you to gain the following ability:

Dual Weapon Specialization: This ability allows the berserker to fight with a one-handed weapon in each hand, and the usual restriction that the offhand weapon must be shorter than the main weapon does not apply. Technically, this can be a shield. When wielding two weapons, you gain an extra Action Point that can be used with the offhand weapon to Parry or make 1 additional Attack. This Bonus attack suffers no additional penalty and achieves any Special Effect normally allowed the main hand weapon.

Upon reaching Rank 3, and each Rank thereafter, an expenditure of Experience Rolls equal to the current Rank and 1 month of training allows you to gain the following:

Improved Berserk Rage: The berserker can Rage once per day for each level taken at no Fatigue loss.

Monk Changes
The following changes to the Monk class apply to all Abilities and Talents, keeping the monk relevant at higher ranks.

Implementation Time: The number of abilities/talents that the monk can prepare with a single Mysticism roll is equal to their current Rank. A rank 3 monk could prepare 3 abilities/talents. The time to implement the them is based on the single ability/talent with the greatest augmentation.

For example, a Rank 2 monk that wished to Augment both Unarmed (a Rank 1 ability) to Easy, and Evade (a Rank 2 ability) to Very Easy, could do so with a single Mysticism roll. The time to implement the talents is based on Evade with its 2 points of Intensity. The monk would need to use 2 Cast Magic Actions to finish. If he had chosen to augment them both to Easy (one Intensity each), it could have been done with a single Cast Magic Action.

Costs of Implementing a Talent: The cost in Magic Points is unchanged. In the above example, 3 Magic Points are spent as usual.

Invoke Traits: Both Slowfall and Arrowcut possesses an Instant casting time and can therefore be used as Reactive Actions.

Rules Additions

Ranger Changes

The following is not really a change, but the first bullet point contains a typo, and the second was inadvertently cut from the Ranger write-up. Both fall under Bow/Light Crossbow Specialization.

- The Critical chance when aiming should be equal to 1/5th the character's skill (20%), not 1/20th.
- Add between the first and second paragraph under Bow/Light Crossbow Specialization. "In addition, if not surprised the specialist can automatically fire first (before rolling for initiative) at the beginning of combat, assuming both weapon and ammo are readied."

Thief and Thief-Acrobat Changes

Backstab: This staple of the thief class needs a serious boost to make it the feared attack that it is supposed to be. Please replace the current backstab rules with the following:

Backstab allows a melee attacker to attempt to neutralize a victim from an advantageous position. Contrary to its name, the weapon does not have to be impaling, but only Small and Medium melee weapons can be used. Ranged attacks do not benefit from backstab. Because the attacker is typically able to strike without hindrance, like Surprise, the first attack on the target gains a bonus Special Effect if successful. In addition, the thief can shift their Damage Modifier by one step for every two Ranks they have in Thief or Thief-Acrobat. Therefore, a halfling thief with a -1d2 damage penalty will have no penalty at Rank 1, gain a +1d2 bonus at Rank 3, and gain a +1d4 at Rank 5. It is not necessary for the thief to gain surprise on her victim, however the attack must be made from outside the victim's field of vision. Therefore, many thieves will wait for an opponent to become engaged with an ally, then take advantage of the distraction to strike from behind.

A Rank 1 thief begins with one of the following additional abilities at character creation at no cost. The second ability can be taken at any time, at a cost of 1 Experience Roll and 1 month of training:

Agile: The thief gains superb reflexes. When calculating Initiative the character adds one tenth of his or her Athletics skill to the Initiative 1d10 roll. For example, a thief with Athletics 60% would calculate Initiative on her Initiative base, +1d10+6.

Quick: The thief can add 2m (5 ft.) to her base movement rate. The metre/foot conversion is not exact, being simplified to better work with existing movement modifiers and battle grids.

Becoming a Multi-Class Character

While they are included under *Starting as a Multi-Class Character*, some of the restrictions are missing from the rules for *Becoming a Multi-Class Character*. These are detailed below:

Character Classes

Cavaliers, Monks, Paladins, and Rangers, cannot multi-class.

Ranks and Advancement

The character will only have the Luck Points from the highest ranked class.

Magic

Acquisition of New Divine Spells

Divine spell casters are at a severe disadvantage when compared to their Arcane counterparts with regards to acquiring new spells, as they do not have the ability to learn them from spell books nor scrolls. This means that their most common method of acquisition is through the expenditure of Experience Rolls, slowing their spell growth considerably. This additional rule offers better balance for the spell casting classes.

When a divine spell caster finishes the required period of prayer and devotion to learn new Divine magic, but before spending the requisite number of Experience Rolls, they should make a Piety skill check. Assuming the roll succeeds, they are granted the desired spell for 1 less Experience Roll, while a critical success grants the spell for 2 fewer Experience Rolls. A failed skill roll still grants the spell as normal, however there is no reduction in Experience Rolls, while a fumble results in a different spell than that desired by the caster being granted by their deity, as chosen by the Games Master. In this case, the spell can be of a different Rank as well. The Piety skill roll cannot reduce the point expenditure below 1, instead granting an additional spell of any usable Rank for each additional point the roll would reduce the Experience cost. For example, reducing the cost to 0 would grant one additional spell, and reducing the cost to -1 would grant 2 additional spells. These additional spells are a gift from the character's deity as a reward for their piety and service, and therefore should be chosen by the Games Master.

Monster Summoning (All Versions)

In a situation where the randomly determined monsters are summoned into an area where sufficient room does not exist, the spell automatically fails. Thus attempting to cast the higher rank versions of the spell in a typical dungeon corridor and getting a young adult dragon result, is typically not beneficial.

Spell Casting Modifiers (Ranks 4-5)

The CLASSIC FANTASY Expert Set includes a sample of Rank 4 and 5 spells for high level gameplay. These are very powerful and difficult to cast successfully, with the relevant spell casting roll being Hard in the case of Rank 4 spells, and Formidable for those of Rank 5.

For example, after years of adventure, Rengarth has attained Rank 4 and can finally cast Rank 4 spells. His Arcane Casting skill is 110%, which applies to all his Rank 1 to 3 spells, however, when casting his newly acquired Rank 4 spells, his chance of success is reduced to 74% (2/3rd of 110 = 73.2, rounded up). Later, after years of further adventuring, Rengarth has finally attained Rank 5, with an Arcane Casting of 130%. All Rank 4 spells would have an 87% chance to cast (2/3rd of 130 = 86.4 rounded up), and Rank 5 spells would be cast at only 65% (1/2 of 130 = 65).

Due to the high initial skill levels, this system doesn't work appropriately if using the Simplified Difficulty Grades. It is suggested that if using this system, the Difficulty Grades of Hard and Formidable be changed to -40 and -60 respectively with regards to the casting of Rank 4 and 5 spells. The normal modifiers are used in all other situations.

For example, having attained Rank 4 with an Arcane Casting skill of 110%, Rengarth has his chance of success reduced to 70% (110 -40 = 70) when casting Rank 4 spells. Later, after attaining Rank 5 and a skill of 130%, his chance to cast Rank 4 spells would be 90% (130 -40 = 90), and Rank 5 spells would be cast at only 70% (130 -60 = 70).

New Arcane Spells

Rank 4

Control Weather
(Alteration)

Cost: 3, +1/Intensity

Area: 1d4x1.5 km (1d4 square miles)/Intensity

Casting Time: 10 Minutes

Duration: 1d6 Hours/Intensity

Range: 0

Resist: NA

This spell allows the caster to alter the current weather in a significant and noticeable way. Once cast, another 1d4x10 Minutes must pass for the effects to completely manifest. The caster can alter the Precipitation, Temperature, and Wind by up to plus or minus two grades as detailed on the tables on page 85 of MYTHRAS. See the Temperature Table on page 327 of CLASSIC FANTASY to translate from Celsius to Fahrenheit. The duration of any change is calculated according to the spell's Intensity, as opposed to that noted on the tables.

Death Spell
(Necromancy)

Cost: 3, +1/Intensity, +1 EXP

Area: 4m (15 ft) Radius

Casting Time: 2 Actions

Duration: Instantaneous

Range: 10m (30 ft)/Intensity

Resist: Endurance

The successful casting of this spell kills a variable number of creatures SIZ 40 or less in the area of effect, assuming they possess a Rank not greater than 3 if applicable. The magic-user rolls 1d6 for each level of Intensity to determine the number of creatures affected. Larger or higher rank creatures count as multiple creatures in this regard. Where creatures of differing sizes occupy the area of effect, smaller creatures are always affected before larger ones. The chance to resist the spell, along with the modifier to the number of creatures affected, is based on their Rank or SIZ, whichever gives the more beneficial result – as summarised below.

DEATH SPELL

Target Rank	Target SIZ	Endurance Modifier	Results
0-1*	1-20	Standard	Each creature counts as 1
2	21-30	Easy	Each creature counts as 2
3	31-40	Very Easy	Each creature counts as 5
4-5	41+	No effect	No Effect

* This category includes characters that do not possess a class.

Casting the spell at sufficient Intensity to equal or exceed the number of potential targets is desirable, as insufficient points are lost. This spell has no effect on lycanthropes, undead, or other planar creatures. Only a Wish can bring those affected by this spell back from the dead.

Example: Rengarth casts the Death Spell into an area occupied by four SIZ 16 orcs and two SIZ 32 hill giants, choosing an Intensity of 3. Rolling 3d6 for the spells effects, 1d6 per Intensity, results in 12 points. While each hill giant requires only 5 points to be killed, the smaller orcs are the first affected. Three of the four orcs fail their Resistance roll and succumb to death. As each orc is equal to 1 point, 8 points remain. This is enough to affect a single hill giant for 5 points, with the remaining 3 points being lost. However, the hill giant has no problem succeeding at its Very Easy Resistance roll and charges at Rengarth.

Fire Ball (Delayed Blast)
(Evocation)

Cost: 3, +1/Intensity

Area: 6m (20 ft) Radius

Casting Time: 2 Actions

Duration: See Below
Range: 15m (50 ft)/Intensity
Resist: Evade

With the exceptions noted both above and in the following text, this spell functions as per the normal Fireball spell. The Delayed Blast Fireball inflicts damage according to the Spell Damage Table based on Intensity, however at one additional grade. When cast, the magic-user can set the Fireball to detonate at any time between instantly and within five minutes. It traverses to the designated spot and then remains inert until the desired time, when it flashes back into existence in a massive ball of flame.

Flesh to Stone (Reversible)
(Alteration)

Cost: 3/Intensity
Area: One Target
Casting Time: 2 Actions
Duration: Permanent
Range: 10m (30 ft)/Intensity
Resist: Willpower

When cast, one victim within range is allowed a Willpower Resistance Roll. If unsuccessful, the victim and all carried and worn belongings are completely transformed into solid stone. This transformation is not death, but instead a form of suspended animation. The casting of either the reversed version of this spell, or a Wish, can be used to restore the victim to life once again. Any damage the victim suffers while stoned carries over, taking effect immediately upon restoration.

Larger creatures are less susceptible to this spell, finding it easier to resist. This is detailed in the following table.

The reverse of this spell, Stone to Flesh, is used to restore a victim and no roll to resist is necessary. However, the spell can also be reversed to transform stone that was never previously alive, being used in one of several creative ways. For example, a wall of stone 3 cubic metres (10 cubic feet) in size per level of Intensity can be

Flesh to Stone

SIZ	Resistance Roll Difficulty
1-20	Standard
21-40	Easy
41+	Very Easy

transformed into soft flesh, a 'tunnel' of flesh up to 1 metre (3 feet) wide, with a length of 3 metres (10 feet) per Intensity could be created, a single target such as a stone statue could be transformed into a body, and even a stone golem could be transformed into a flesh golem by means of this spell. However, in the latter case the stone golem would be allowed a Willpower roll to resist as normal. Stone turned to flesh in this way is soft and pliable, and while it retains its actual hit points, possesses no armour points, thus making it easier to hack apart.

Globe of Invulnerability
(Abjuration)

Cost: 3, +1/Intensity
Area: 1.5m (5 ft) Radius
Casting Time: 1 Round
Duration: 1 Minute/Intensity
Range: 0
Resist: NA

The casting of this spell creates a magical sphere of faintly shimmering energy around the caster, offering complete protection from all Rank 1-3 spells. Area effect spells that originate from outside of the sphere can engulf it, but fail to penetrate its radius. The exception is Dispel Magic, which if cast at sufficient Intensity will cause it to collapse. Active spell-like abilities possessed by magical items and creatures, such as those that mimic an arcane or divine spell's effects, also prevent entry, as do creatures under the effects of Rank 1-3 spells until those effects are dropped. This does not affect a monk's mystical talents however. Those wearing magic items with an Intensity less than that of the Globe of Invulnerability will be stopped at the point of contact if entering, but can leave unhindered.

Invisible Stalker
(Summoning)

Cost: 3, +1 EXP, Plus See Below
Area: See Below
Casting Time: 1 Round
Duration: See Below
Range: 10m (30 ft)
Resist: NA/Willpower

This spell summons a 4-cubic metre air elemental to carry out whatever task the magic-user puts before it. This specific elemental is known as an invisible stalker, a tireless entity that accurately tracks and pursues prey without fail. Invisible stalkers understand the Common Tongue, but speak only their own Language (Air Elemental) INT+CHA +40. Any task assigned to them is carried out without question, regardless of the command or how long it takes. However, the stalker does this not out of loyalty, but servitude. Therefore, complex requests or lengthy tasks will be resented, granting the stalker a chance to resist with an Opposed Willpower roll. A successful roll on its part frees it of its servitude, where it will return to the elemental plane. If the stalker's assigned mission is to continue, the +1 EXP listed in the spell's cost must be paid every time Experience Rolls are awarded, or the creature is free of its bonds and escapes back to the elemental plane.

Monster Summoning, Greater
(Summoning)

Cost: 3, +1/additional Intensity
Area: 46m (150 ft) Radius
Casting Time: 2 Rounds
Duration: 6 Minutes/Intensity
Range: 0
Resist: NA

This spell functions in all ways as the Rank 2 version except where it differs as noted above. The monsters summoned are drawn from the Level 5 Dungeon Monsters Table.

Reincarnation, Arcane
(Necromancy)

Cost: 3, +1/additional Intensity, +1 EXP
Area: One Target
Casting Time: 10 Minutes
Duration: Permanent
Range: Touch
Resist: See Below

This spell is cast while touching the corpse of a creature dead less than 24 hours per level of Intensity. However, this version of Reincarnation has no effect on full-blooded elves (instead, see Divine Reincarnation). If the victim's Ethical Passion was anything other than evil, the victim resists the spell with an Opposed Willpower Roll, and if successful, negates the effects of the spell. This is because the soul or spirit of the deceased is rarely willing to enter a new body once it has reached its eternal reward. The Games Master can decide to waive the roll if the recipient has unfinished business, cannot be separated from their true love, or has some other heroic reason to live. In the case of evil souls, who would gladly return instead of suffering eternal damnation, it isn't the deceased's Willpower that's resisting, but that of the demon, devil, etc., placed in charge of their punishment, their tormentor. In this case, the caster must overcome the tormentor's Willpower. If this is unknown, assume it is at least 20 points higher than that of the deceased to represent that the stronger the soul's will, the more powerful the being placed in charge of his or her damnation. If the caster succeeds, they have successfully anchored the spirit to the host. While a failed roll results in the victim being either unwilling or unable to return.

If the casting is successful, a fully formed adult body appears in 1d6x10 minutes containing the consciousness of the deceased. The caster has no control of the form or sex in which the soul returns, although the former character class and rank is retained. This means it may take some convincing on the part of the character that they are who they say they are when dealing with friends, family, and former acquaintances; and includes their order or guild when it comes time for advancement if relevant. This is best represented by Influence rolls on the part of the character, modified by how drastic the change, as determined by the Games Master. For example, a dwarf reincarnated into another dwarf may require a standard Influence roll to convince a former ally of their actual identity, while being reincarnated into a gnome or halfling could result in the roll being one grade more difficult. Finally, that same character could find it two grades more difficult convincing others of their identity if changed into something as extreme as a goblin, orc, or troll.

Roll on the Reincarnation table to determine the new form.

All characteristics are determined randomly as per the new form, with the exception of INT, POW, and CHA which remain unchanged. Recalculate the character's Base skill levels and adjust

Reincarnation, Arcane

D100	Reincarnation Result
01-20	Human
21-60	Demi-Human
	01-20: Dwarf
	21-40: Elf
	41-60: Gnome
	61-80: Half-Elf
	81-00: Halfling
61-95	Humanoid/Monster
	01-10: Bugbear
	11-26: Gnoll
	27-42: Goblin
	43-58: Hobgoblin
	59-74: Kobold
	75-90: Orc
	91-95: Ogre
	96-00: Troll
96-00	Other, GM's Option

the skill totals accordingly. Passions are unaffected. Any former racial abilities are lost and replaced with those of the new species. If the new form is unsuited to the old character class, the only option is to deal with it, or learn a new class. The reincarnated individual remembers most of their former life, though the Games Master can ask for the character to make a Willpower roll to remember significant facts for the first week. A Wish can return the reincarnated individual back to their previous form if later desired.

True Seeing
(Divination)

Cost: 3, +1/Intensity

Area: 1 Target

Casting Time: 1 Round

Duration: 1 Minute/Intensity

Range: Touch

Resist: NA

True Seeing grants the subject the ability to see the world clearly, to a range of 18m (60 ft), subject to Line of Sight. All secrets within the area of effect become apparent; both natural and magical darkness is penetrated; secret doors become visible; invisible or ethereal attackers are revealed; illusions and phantasms become obvious; and the true form of shape-changed creatures is revealed. Even the ethereal and other planes adjacent to the material plane can be glimpsed with Concentration, as defined on page 127 of Classic Fantasy. True Seeing also negates the effects of spells such as Blur and Mirror Image. In addition to mundane material components, casting True Seeing requires Rare ingredients made from powdered mushrooms, saffron, and animal fat, with a value of at least 300 GP.

Word of Power - Blind
(Summoning)

Cost: 3, +1/additional Intensity

Area: 4m (15 ft) Radius

Casting Time: 1 Action

Duration: See Below

Range: 6m (20 ft)/Intensity

Resist: Willpower

Upon successfully casting this spell, one creature of the caster's choice within both line of sight and range, is selected as the epicenter. This target and all others in a 4m (15 ft) radius are struck blind upon failing their roll to resist. This blindness can be cured by the casting of Cure Blindness or Dispel Magic. The chance to resist the spell, along with its duration, is modified by the target's Rank or SIZ, whichever gives the more beneficial result. This is detailed on the following table.

WORD OF POWER - BLIND

Target Rank	Target SIZ	Willpower Modifier	Duration
0-1*	1-20	Formidable	1d4+1 x10 minutes**
2	21-40	Hard	1d4+1 minutes
3	41-60	Standard	1d4+1 rounds
4	61-80	Easy	1d3 rounds
5	81+	Very Easy	1 round

* *This category includes characters that do not possess a class.*

** *If only one to three creatures are in the area of effect, the effects are permanent until magically treated.*

Rank 5

Astral Spell
(Alteration)

Cost: 3, +1/additional Intensity

Area: See Below

Casting Time: 2 Actions

Duration: See Below

Range: Touch

Resist: NA

This spell allows the caster and up to five others (one per additional level of Intensity) to enter the Astral Plane using a method very similar to psychic astral travel. All must be touching and forming a circle while the spell is cast. The traveller's bodies are left behind in the plane of origin, and they typically do not bring with them any clothing or equipment with the exception of that which itself radiates a magical aura. These items transform into astral equivalents of their normal form. A silver cord of spiritual energy connects the travellers to their bodies; however, after a length of 3 metres (10 feet), the cords become both intangible and invisible. The duration lasts until the caster wills it to cease. However, it is possible for it to be ended prematurely by an outside force such as Dispel Magic. Killing the caster's physical body also ends the spell early, although this has the unfortunate side effect of stranding any travellers accompanying the caster. See page 307 of Classic Fantasy for more information on astral travel.

New Arcane Spells

Mass Charm
(Enchantment (Charm))

Cost: 3/Intensity, +1 EXP
Area: 6m (20 ft) Radius/Intensity
Casting Time: 2 Rounds
Duration: 1 Week/Intensity
Range: 12m (40 ft)/Intensity

Resist: Willpower

With the exceptions noted both above, this spell functions as per the spells Charm Being and Charm Monster. This most powerful of charm spells has a chance to charm all creatures within the area of effect. Each victim's chance to resist is based on their SIZ, as for the normal lesser version of the spell, however, the chance is one grade more difficult due to its more potent nature. Unlike other charm spells, there is no limit placed on the size of the victim. This is summarised in the following table.

Mass Charm

SIZ	Resistance Roll Modifier
1-20	One grade harder
21-40	Standard difficulty
41+	One grade easier

Meteor Shower
(Evocation)

Cost: 3/Intensity
Area: See Below
Casting Time: 2 Actions
Duration: Instantaneous
Range: 18m (20 ft)/Intensity

Resist: Evade

When the magic-user casts this spell, two micro-meteors per level of Intensity streak from her outstretched hand. The meteors arc towards their target, impacting on a downward trajectory, leaving a trail of sparks and cinders in their wake. Upon impact, they detonate in multiple fiery explosions around the target point. The first meteor always strikes the targeted location, while any additional meteors strike randomly around it, each with an explosive radius of 3 metres (10 feet). To determine where they hit, roll 1d8 for the direction, consulting the diagram for "Missing with a Thrown Weapon" on page 111 of Classic Fantasy. The missiles each impact 1d6-1 x1.5 metres (1d6-1 x5 feet) from the initial strike. Each meteor does 1d6 points of fire damage to those in the area of effect and requires the target to succeed at an Athletics roll to remain standing. However, due to the radius of each explosion, many will overlap, doing additional damage to those unfortunate enough to get caught by them. In this case, add the damage of each overlapping area together, and increase the Difficulty of the Athletics roll by one step for each overlapping explosion.

This damage is applied to each hit location, with Armour Points counting as half normal. Magic armour applies its entire magic bonus. On a successful Resistance roll the victim suffers half the rolled damage. Meteor Shower has a chance of igniting flammable materials. See 'Fires' in Chapter 6 of Classic Fantasy for additional information.

Monster Summoning, Ultimate
(Summoning)

Cost: 3, +1/additional Intensity
Area: 60m (200 ft) Radius
Casting Time: 2 Rounds
Duration: 10 Minutes/Intensity
Range: 0

Resist: NA

This spell functions in all ways as the Rank 2 version except where it differs as noted above. The monsters summoned are drawn from the Level 7 Dungeon Monsters Table on pages 29-30.

Word of Power - Kill
(Summoning)

Cost: 3/Intensity, +1 EXP
Area: 3m (10 ft) Radius
Casting Time: 1 Action
Duration: Permanent
Range: 6m (20 ft)/Intensity

Resist: Willpower

The successful casting of this spell has a chance to kill either a single creature of 20 SIZ per Intensity, to a maximum of SIZ 80, or 5 creatures per Intensity, each no larger than SIZ 20. All potential targets must lie within the area of effect, as designated when the spell is cast. The chance to resist the spell is modified by the target's Rank or SIZ, whichever gives the more beneficial result, as detailed on the following table.

Word of Power - Kill

Target Rank	Target SIZ	Willpower Modifier
0-1*	1-20	Formidable
2	21-40	Hard
3	41-60	Standard
4	61-80	Easy
5	81+	No effect

This category includes characters that do not possess a class.

Creatures in excess of SIZ 80 are unaffected, as are characters of Rank 5. Unlike the Death Spell, Word of Power will kill anything within the above-mentioned limits, however, it is possible to bring victims back to life through the casting of Wish, Raise Dead, Resurrection, and Reincarnation as normal.

Time Stop
(Alteration)

Cost: 3, +1/additional Intensity, +1 EXP
Area: 4m (15 ft) Radius
Casting Time: 2 Actions
Duration: See Below
Range: 0

Resist: NA

With the casting of this spell, time stands still for all except the caster and one other character within the area of effect for each additional level of Intensity. The caster rolls 1d3 to determine the relative duration of the spell in minutes, as perceived by the magic-user and any chosen allies or other individuals. During this time, they can move about the area of effect, although leaving the spell's radius negates it early. They are free to operate as desired within the radius, including casting spells or dispatching enemies, but anything done that passes beyond the area of effect also negates the spell. It is permissible to teleport from the area of effect, but this also negates the spell. When time is once again set in motion, those caught in the area of effect need to make a Formidable Perception roll to notice the effects of the spell.

New Divine Spells

Rank 4

Animal Growth (Reversible)
(Alteration)

Sphere: Animal

Cost: 3, +1/additional Intensity

Area: 3m (10 ft) Radius

Casting Time: 2 Actions

Duration: 2 Minutes/Intensity

Range: 75m (250 ft)

Resist: NA

This spell causes up to 2 animals per Intensity in the area of effect to increase to twice their normal size. For the purposes of the spell, an animal is defined as any non-sapient, non-magical creature, easily classified as a bird, reptile, mammal, fish, etc. It therefore has no effect on creatures possessing the INT characteristic rather than INS, nor on supernatural or magical creatures like pegasi, dragons, or basilisks. This spell effectively doubles the recipients SIZ characteristic, while increasing their STR by half again the norm. Attributes such as Damage Modifier and Hit Points will need to be reevaluated, and the Games Master should refer to Default Natural Weapons for Unusually Sized Creatures on page 222 of MYTHRAS to adjust the creature's base damage, size, and reach of its attacks if necessary. Because most of the creature's physical skills are based on muscle memory, they need not be adjusted, nor is the creature's Armour Points or Movement effected.

When reversed, Animal Diminishment reduces the SIZ of 2 animals per Intensity in the area of effect to half normal, decreasing SIZ and STR by half. All other effects are the inverse of the above information.

Animal Summoning II
(Conjuration)

Sphere: Animal

Cost: 3, +1/Intensity

Area: 1 km (.5 mi.) Radius/Intensity

Casting Time: 1 Round

Duration: See Below

Range: 0

Resist: NA

With the exceptions noted above and in the following text, this spell functions as per Animal Summoning I. The maximum combined SIZ of all the animals that answer the summons is equal to spell's Intensity x12; therefore, if cast at Intensity 3 (total SIZ 36), the spell could summon four SIZ 8 Wolves (total SIZ 32), two SIZ 17 boars (total SIZ 34), or one SIZ 34 bear. The animals summoned are limited to a maximum SIZ of 60 and, regardless of number, no more than eight will respond. Each additional level of Intensity beyond the first extends the range of the spell another kilometre (half mile), which in turn decreases the casting Difficulty 1 Grade.

Animate Object
(Alteration)

Sphere: Creation, Summoning

Cost: 1/Intensity

Area: 6 HP/Intensity

Casting Time: 2 Actions

Duration: 1 Minute/Intensity

Range: 30m (100 ft)

Resist: NA

Through the use of this spell, the caster imbues a normally inert, inorganic object with mobility. The object can only be animated if it already possesses a form that would promote locomotion, such as a chair with its four legs, a humanoid statue, a bottle that rolls on the floor, a rope that slithers across the ground like a snake, and so on. While there is typically no Resistance Roll regarding the animation

Common Dungeon Object Table

Object	Size	Reach	Damage	Combat Effects	Armour Points	Hit Points	Move Method	Move
Barrel, Empty	M	T	1d4	Bash, Stun Location	4	9	Roll	4m (15 ft)
Barrel, Full	M	T	1d4	Bash, Stun Location	6	9	Roll	4m (15 ft)
Boulder, SIZ 12	M	T	1d8+1d6	Bash, Stun Location	10	20	Roll	3m (10 ft)
Boulder, SIZ 25	L	T	2d8+1d8+1d6	Bash, Stun Location	10	40	Roll	3m (10 ft)
Boulder, SIZ 50	H	T	3d8+2d10+1d2	Bash, Stun Location	10	60	Roll	1.5m (5 ft)
Boulder, SIZ 75	E	T	4d8+2d10+1d8	Bash, Stun Location	10	80	Roll	1.5m (5 ft)
Brazier, Metal	S	T	1d8	Bash, Stun Location, Fire*	8	12	Walk	6m (20 ft)
Chain, 2m (6 ft)	S	M	1d4	Bash, Entangle	8	8	Slither	1.5m (5 ft)
Chair/Stool	S	S	1d6	Bash, Stun Location	2	6	Walk	6m (20 ft)
Throne	M-L	T	1d6+1d10	Bash, Stun Location	6	25	Walk	4m (15 ft)
Pedestal, Stone	S-M	T	1d8	Bash, Stun Location	10	10	Wobble	3m (10 ft)
Pedestal, Wood	S-M	T	1d6	Bash, Stun Location	4	8	Wobble	4m (15 ft)
Rope, 3m (10 ft)	S	L	1d2	Stun Location, Entangle	6	3	Slither	3m (10 ft)
Rug, 2 x 3m (6x10 ft)	M	M	1d2	Bash, Stun Location	6	6	Slither	1.5m (5 ft)
Metal Statue, Giant-Sized	E	L	2d8+2d8	Bash, Grip, Stun Location**	10	42	Walk	3m (10 ft)
Metal Statue, Man-Sized	H	M	1d8+1d8	Bash, Grip, Stun Location**	10	21	Walk	4m (15 ft)
Stone Statue, Giant-Sized	E	L	2d8+1d8+1d6	Bash, Grip, Stun Location**	10	36	Walk	3m (10 ft)
Stone Statue, Man-Sized	L	M	1d8+1d6	Bash, Grip, Stun Location**	8	18	Walk	4m (15 ft)
Wood Statue, Giant-Sized	M	M	2d6+1d12	Bash, Grip, Stun Location**	6	30	Walk	4m (15 ft)
Wood Statue, Man-Sized	M	M	1d6+1d4	Bash, Grip, Stun Location**	4	15	Walk	6m (20 ft)
Suit of Plate Armour	M	M	1d8	Bash, Grip, Stun Location**	6-8	4	Walk	6m (20 ft)
Table, 1x1m (3x3 ft)	M	S	1d6	Bash, Stun Location	4	12	Walk	6m (20 ft)
Table, 1x2m (3x6 ft)	L	S	1d6+1d6	Bash, Stun Location	4	18	Walk	4m (15 ft)
Table, 1.5x4m (5x15 ft)	H	S	1d6+1d12	Bash, Stun Location	4	30	Walk	3m (10 ft)

* Can set fire to the target

** May possess additional Combat Effects if armed

of objects, items currently being held by a creature allow the creature a Willpower roll to resist. Each level of Intensity animates up to 6 Hit Points, and grants the target attributes based on the object. See the accompanying Common Dungeon Object Table as well at the Initiative and Action Point Table for further information. To determine Damage Modifier, calculate twice the objects Hit Points and consult the Damage Modifier Table in MYTHRAS, ignoring a Damage Penalty. Body Locations are not used, with a particular object being destroyed when reduced to 0 Hit Points. However, reducing an object to ½ its total Hit Points is usually enough to render it immobile, dispelling the enchantment.

New Divine Spells

Initiative and Action Point Table

Material	Init.	AP
Flexible; Rope, Chain, etc.	20	3
Wood	15	3
Metal, Articulated	15	2
Metal, Solid	10	2
Stone	10	2

The caster imbues the objects with INS based on 1/10th Arcane Casting skill. This total is divided between each as desired when the items are animated. Therefore, a single animated object possesses a higher INS than several. An animated object can be commanded to perform a single task for each point of INS; such as patrol the corridors, attack intruders, hold the door, etc. Unless the assigned tasks are ongoing, the object performs them once, and then stands idle until commanded again.

See Inanimate Objects on page 81 of Mythras for more information pertaining to attacking objects, which weapons to use, which not to use, etc.

Commune
(Divination)

Sphere: Divination
Cost: 3/Intensity
Area: See Below
Casting Time: 10 Minutes
Duration: See Below
Range: 0
Resist: NA

This spell allows the caster to enter a meditative, trancelike state, and attempt to contact her deity, or one of its representatives. The cleric can ask a single yes or no question per level of Intensity, although, the Games Master may allow a short answer of no more than five words if additional detail is required. Questions are answered truthfully, although as deities in Classic Fantasy are not omnificent, "I'm unsure" is a suitable answer, even if it isn't the one the caster was hoping for. This spell cannot be used to divine a future event, only something that has transpired in the past, or is taking place somewhere in the present. Because the gods value their time and tend to dislike needless interruption, each additional use of this spell within the same month reduces the chance by another grade of difficulty, regardless of whether the former was successful or otherwise, and resets the clock. For example, the second attempt would be Formidable and the third Herculean. A Difficulty Grade of Hopeless means no further attempts are possible, and as each attempt re-sets the clock, a failed third attempt would mean that a month (30 days), needs to transpire before the spell can be used once again.

Control Winds
(Alteration)

Sphere: Weather
Cost: 1/Intensity
Area: 12m (40 ft)/Intensity
Casting Time: 2 Actions
Duration: 10 Minutes/Intensity
Range: 0
Resist: NA

This spell allows the caster to alter the current wind strength in a significant and noticeable way. To do so, a desired wind strength is chosen by the caster, and compared to the current wind strength, as detailed on the Wind Table on page 85 of Mythras. Each point of Intensity can be used to alter the current wind strength as noted on the beforementioned table, by up to plus or minus two grades per Intensity. The change is not instant, with the wind speed changing at a rate of 5 STR per Round until the change designated by the caster is reached. During the spell's duration, the caster simply concentrates to cause the wind to increase, decrease, or remain at its current STR, changing it as desired from Round to Round, however she cannot alter the speed of the change any further. Once the spell's

duration ends, the wind returns to its normal speed at a rate of 5 STR per Round.

An area of calm exists around the caster in a 6 metre (20 foot) radius, and if used in a confined space, such as a great hall, cavern, or dungeon chamber, the area of calm shrinks by 1.5 metres (5 feet) for every full 1.5 metres (5 feet) of restriction on the area of effect. Restricting the spell's area of effect to a sufficient degree eliminates the area of calm completely, subjecting the caster to the wind's effects. The spell can be countered by another use of Control Winds.

Conjure Fire Elemental (Reversible)
(Summoning)

Sphere: Elemental (Fire)

Cost: 3, +1/additional Intensity

Area: See Below

Casting Time: 5 Minutes

Duration: 10 Minutes/Intensity

Range: 75m (250 ft)

Resist: NA

When this spell is cast, an elemental is brought forth from the Elemental Plane of Fire through a gate or portal. This elemental offers no harm to the caster nor their allies, but will defend them and offer any aid required. In addition to returning to its elemental plane upon the end of the spell's duration, the elemental can be banished through Dispel Magic, or the reversed version of this spell, Dismiss Fire Elemental. When reversed, the caster need only cast the spell at a single level of Intensity to complete the dismissal regardless of the Magnitude of the original spell.

CONJURE FIRE ELEMENTAL

D100	Fire Elemental Table
01-65	1 six cubic-metre Fire Elemental
66-90	1 eight cubic-metre Fire Elemental
91-98	1 ten cubic-metre Fire Elemental
99-00	1 twelve cubic-metre Fire Elemental

Dispel Evil (Reversible)
(Abjuration)

Sphere: Protection, Summoning

Cost: 3, +1/additional Intensity

Area: 1 Target

Casting Time: 2 Actions

Duration: 3 Rounds/Intensity

Range: Touch

Resist: Willpower

When this spell is cast, the cleric is imbued with the power to banish evil entities from other planes of existence through contact. This ability passes through any object wielded by the cleric, such as a staff or other melee weapon; however, the entity in contact is allowed a roll to resist the banishment. In addition, all attacks against the cleric by creatures subject to the spell's effects, find their attacks one grade more difficult. As soon as the spell successfully banishes an enemy, its duration expires; otherwise it functions for 3 Rounds per Intensity.

The reverse of the spell, Banish Good, works as detailed above, but only effects good creatures summoned from other planes of existence.

Flame Strike
(Evocation)

Sphere: Combat, Elemental (Fire)

Cost: 3, +1/additional Intensity

Area: 1.5m (5 ft) Radius

Casting Time: 2 Actions

Duration: Instantaneous

Range: 55m (180 ft)

Resist: Evade

Upon successfully casting this spell, a column of flame 10 metres (30 feet) in height streaks down from above, scorching an area designated by the cleric. Those in the area of effect are subjected to damage based on the Spell Damage Table to each hit location, with Armour Points counting as half normal. Magic armour applies its entire Magic Bonus. A successful Resistance roll allows the victim to suffer only half the rolled damage. Flame Strike has a chance of igniting flammable materials. See 'Fires' in Chapter 6 for additional information.

Heal (Reversible)
(Necromancy)

Sphere: Healing

Cost: 3, +1/Intensity

Area: 1 Creature

Casting Time: 1 Minute

Duration: Permanent

Range: Touch

Resist: NA (Endurance)

With the casting of Heal, the cleric cures all disease and injury with a single touch. The actual extent of this recovery is based on the Intensity of the spell as follows. At a single level of Intensity, the spell heals the subject of all disease, cures any blindness and/or deafness, negates mental disorders brought on by injury or magic, and completely heals a single body location of all damage. It will not however, restore a severed limb, that requires a casting of the Rank 5 spell Regenerate. Each additional Intensity completely heals another body location. It would therefore require a casting of Heal at Intensity 7 to completely cure an individual suffering burns to his entire body. Unlike lesser healing spells that limit their effectiveness against long-term injuries, there are no limits placed on the spell by the duration in which the subject has suffered the effects of injury.

When reversed, Harm inflicts magical injury to one of the victim's body locations, reducing it to 1 hit point with a successful Resistance roll on the part of the victim, and -1 on a failed roll. In addition, a malady is inflicted upon them, the effects of which are the same as the reversed Rank 2 Divine spell Cure Disease. Each additional Intensity affects another Body Location contiguous to the first, with effects as determined by the initial Resistance roll. Large creatures (SIZ 21-40) have an easier chance to resist a casting of Harm, with their Resistance roll being Easy, while the Resistance roll for huge creatures (SIZ 41+) is Very Easy. Neither version of this spell has any effect on undead; creatures harmed only by iron, silver, or magical weapons; or beings of a non-corporeal nature.

Insect Plague
(Summoning)

Sphere: Animal, Combat

Cost: 3, +1/additional Intensity

Area: 55m (180 ft) Radius Cloud

Casting Time: 2 Actions

Duration: 2 Rounds/Intensity

Range: 110m (360 ft)

Resist: NA

This spell must be cast somewhere where insects are naturally present. Upon completion, the caster brings forth a thick cloud of nasty flying, crawling, and jumping insects, drawing them from the immediate area. The swarm stays in the area for the duration of the spell, remaining centered on the point designated by the cleric or druid when the spell is cast. Unlike an attack by a normal Insect Swarm, this spell cannot be Evaded; but the swarm cannot pursue victims that leave the area of effect. Those within the spell's area of effect find their vision reduced to only 3 metres (10 feet), and the distraction makes any spell casting of Herculean difficulty. In addition, a Willpower roll is required to resist the urge to flee the area by the fastest way possible, with the victim refusing to stop until at least 150 metres (500 feet) distance is placed between the them and the swarm. The swarm fills a volume 18 metres (60 feet) in height. In all other ways, it functions as an Insect Swarm as detailed on page 251 of Mythras. Insect Plague can be countered with a casting of Dispel Magic of sufficient Intensity. See the following table, which

INSECT PLAGUE

Intensity	SIZ	Random SIZ	Sting/Bite Damage	Combat Actions
1	34-41	33+1d8	1d8	6
2	42-50	42+1d8	1d10	7
3	51-59	51+1d8	1d12	8
4	60-69	61+1d8	2d6	9
5	70-79	71+1d8	1d8+1d6	10

expands on that depicted in Mythras, for the potency of the attack based on Intensity and Swarm SIZ.

Part Water
(Alteration)

Sphere: Elemental (Water)

Cost: 3, +1/additional Intensity

Area: See Below

Casting Time: 10 Minutes

Duration: 10 Minutes/Intensity

Range: 18m (60 ft)/Intensity

Resist: NA

This spell allows the caster to part water or other forms of liquid, creating a safe path which can then be traversed if desired, if cast at sufficient Intensity. The spell creates a trough 30 metres (100 feet) wide, with a depth of 3 metres (10 feet) per Intensity, and a length of 36 metres (120 feet) per Intensity. Therefore, if cast at an Intensity of 7, the parting would be 21 metres (70 feet) deep, 252 metres (840 feet) long, with a width of 30 metres (100 feet). The spell can be ended early by the caster, otherwise it continues until its duration is reached. This spell can be cast underwater, which instead creates a "corridor" of air with the same dimensions noted above. Finally, Part Water can be cast offensively on a creature such as a water elemental, and if so, causes damage equal to three times that found on the Spell Damage Table on page 124 of Classic Fantasy. Assuming the entity survives, it must succeed at a Willpower Resistance roll or flee the caster for 3d4 minutes.

Plane Shift
(Alteration)

Sphere: Astral

Cost: 3, +1/additional Intensity

Area: See Below

Casting Time: 2 Actions

Duration: Permanent

Range: Touch

Resist: Willpower

This spell allows the caster and up to seven others (one per additional level of Intensity) to travel to another plane of existence. All must be touching and forming a circle while the spell is cast. The caster can also use the spell to transport one creature independent of herself, whether willing or otherwise, to a plane of her choice, however the latter is allowed a Willpower roll to resist, with the spell being negated on a successful roll. The precise point of arrival is seldom that desired by the caster. If using a hex map, roll 1d6 to determine the direction, and determine the distance by rolling 1d10x15 kilometres (1d10x10 miles). In addition to any generic material components, the casting of Plane Shift requires a special rod, each constructed of a various rare metals, and each specially attuned to a single plane of existence. These rods are rare, and valued at as much as 5,000 GP each. See Chapter 14 of CLASSIC FANTASY for more information on the various planes of existence.

Raise Dead (Reversible)

(Necromancy)

Sphere: Necromantic

Cost: 3, +1/additional Intensity, +1 EXP

Area: One Target

Casting Time: 1 Minute

Duration: Permanent

Range: 30m (100 ft)

Resist: NA (Willpower)

This spell is cast while touching the corpse of a creature dead less than 24 hours per level of Intensity. Raise Dead is effective on most creatures, however it has no effect on full blooded elves, as only the Rank 5 spell, Resurrection can raise an elf from death. If the subject's Ethical Passion was anything other than evil, they can resist the spell with an Opposed Willpower Roll and, if successful, negate the effects of the spell. This is because the soul or spirit of the deceased is rarely willing to return to the living once it has reached its eternal reward. The Games Master can decide to waive the roll if the recipient has unfinished business, cannot be separated from their true love, or has some other heroic reason to live. In the case of evil souls, who would gladly return instead of suffering eternal damnation, it isn't the deceased's Willpower that's resisting, but that of the demon, devil, etc., placed in charge of their punishment, their tormentor. In this case, the caster must overcome the tormentor's Willpower. If this is unknown, assume it is at least 20 points higher than that of the deceased to represent that the stronger the soul's will, the more powerful the being placed in charge of his or her damnation. If the caster succeeds, they have successfully returned the spirit to the body. While a failed roll results in the victim being either unwilling or unable to return.

If the casting is successful, the subject is returned to life with full hit points, although severed limbs remain lost. This means that a victim decapitated or cut in half cannot be raised until their head or torso is first reattached. This can be done before the casting of Raise Dead by physically reattaching the severed location, which requires a healer's kit and a successful application of the Healing skill, and typically leaves a very obvious and telling scar. Other maladies, such as poison or disease must be taken care of prior to, or after the casting of Raise Dead, or the results are only temporary. Finally, Raise Dead has no effect on a creature that has reached the end of its natural life span, and died of old age.

The act of being raised from the dead is very straining on the subject, who is reduced to a Fatigue Level of Incapacitated for a period of 24 hours for each day they were dead. The casting of Cure Fatigue has no effect on the patient during this time of convalescence. After this point, the character recovers from Fatigue normally, and without restriction.

When reversed, Slay Living, can be used to kill one victim designated by the cleric at the time of the casting. This victim is allowed a Willpower roll to resist, modified by the target's Rank or SIZ, whichever gives the more beneficial result, as detailed on the following table.

If the Resistance roll is unsuccessful, the victim is slain outright. A successful roll is treated as per the effects of Cause Serious Wounds. Armour offers no protection from this damage.

SLAY LIVING

Target Rank	Target SIZ	Willpower Modifier
0-1*	1-20	Hard
2	21-40	Standard
3	41-60	Easy
4-5	61+	Very Easy

* This category includes characters that do not possess a class.

Rock to Mud (Reversible)

(Alteration)

Sphere: Elemental (Earth, Water)

Cost: 3, +1/additional Intensity

Area: 3m (10 ft) Radius/Intensity

Casting Time: 2 Actions

Duration: See Below

Range: 150m (500 ft)

Resist: NA

The casting of this spell transforms all natural stone in the area of effect into soft mud to a depth of 3 metres (10 feet). It has no effect on magical stone, or natural stone given magical properties (such as stone golems or earth elementals). Those unable to escape the mud sink at a rate of 1/3rd their SIZ per minute, and begin to suffer the effects of asphyxiation when completely sunk unless aid is provided in some way. Creatures large enough to touch bottom and still keep their head above the mud, can move at a rate of 1.5m (5 feet) per round, or double with a successful Athletics roll.

The mud transforms into dirt naturally after a period of 1d6 days for every 3 square metres (10 sq. feet) of mud created. However, this process can be expedited with Dispel Magic or Mud to Rock.

When reversed, Mud to Rock hardens mud or quicksand into soft stone such as limestone, sandstone, etc. This change is permanent unless dispelled or subjected to a later casting of Rock to Mud. Creatures in the mud or quicksand are allowed one additional attempt to escape before the mud is transformed, via a successful Brawn or Formidable Evade roll (assuming a possible method of escape exists) to avoid becoming trapped permanently.

True Seeing (Reversible)
(Divination)

Sphere: Divination
Cost: 3, +1/Intensity
Area: One Target
Casting Time: 2 Actions
Duration: 1 Minute/Intensity
Range: Touch
Resist: NA

With the exceptions noted above and as follows, True Seeing functions as per the Arcane spell of the same name. The subject is able to see secrets out to 36m (120 ft), subject to Line of Sight. In addition, creatures viewed display an aura, allowing the subject of the spell to discern their ethical passion; good, neutral, or evil. Finally, the Divine version of True Seeing may be reversed.

When reversed, False Seeing, causes the victim to experience things that are not there, and to see the opposite of what is true. Good is identified as evil, that which is hideous appears beautiful, stairs are easily missed, labeled potions are gibberish, etc. In addition to mundane material components, the casting of False Seeing requires Rare ingredients made from poppy dust, essence of pink orchid, and special oils, all with a value of at least 300 GP.

Weather Summoning
(Summoning)

Sphere: Weather
Cost: 3, +1/Intensity
Area: See Below
Casting Time: 10 Minutes
Duration: See Below
Range: 0
Resist: NA

This spell allows the caster to summon weather appropriate to the current season, climate, and region, and can be anything that occurs normally. This weather change is not controllable by the caster after it is made manifest, and runs its natural course, lasting as little as ten minutes for conditions such as a tornado or summer shower, to as long as days or even weeks for conditions such as a heat wave or cold spell. Similarly, the area of effect can vary accordingly, from as little as 1.5 kilometres (1 mile), to one hundred times that size. Some examples are noted below:

Spring: High or low temperatures, sleet, thunderstorms, tornados, hurricane force winds (early spring, coastal), etc.

Summer: Heat wave, hail storm, heavy rains, etc.

Fall: High or low temperatures, fog, sleet, high winds, etc.

Winter: Freezing cold, thaw conditions, snow storm, blizzard, hurricane force winds (late winter, coastal), etc.

Once cast, within 1d4x10 Minutes the nature of the coming weather change starts to become apparent, with black clouds forming overhead, winds picking up, temperature dropping etc. During this time, the spell can be negated by Dispel Magic of sufficient Intensity, causing the weather to revert back to normal. Otherwise, 1d12+5, x10 minutes after the casting, the weather change comes into full effect. See pages 84-85 of MYTHRAS for details of using weather effects in your game, as well as the Temperature Table on page 327 of CLASSIC FANTASY to translate from Celsius to Fahrenheit where necessary.

Rank 5

Animate Rock
(Alteration)

Sphere: Elemental (Earth)
Cost: 3, +1/additional Intensity
Area: See Below
Casting Time: 1 Round
Duration: 1 Minute/Intensity
Range: 36m (120 ft)
Resist: NA

With the exceptions noted above and as follows, this spell functions as per the Rank 4 spell Animate Object. Animate Rock only affects a single stone object, with each Intensity animating up to 24 Hit Points, or 3 cu. metre (10 cu. ft) of solid stone. A boulder typically possesses 10 Armour Points, while other objects typically possess 8-10. Stone objects animated with this spell have an Initiative Bonus of 10 and 2 Action Points. The stone must be a single object such as a boulder or statue; partial pieces of stone cannot be affected individually. However, a large statue mounted on a stone base is allowed to break free if commanded to do so. Stone objects animated with

Animate Rock

Object	Size	Reach	Damage	Combat Effects	Armour Points	Hit Points	Movement Method	Movement
Boulder, SIZ 12	M	T	1d8+1d6	Bash, Stun Location	10	20	Roll	3m (10 ft)
Boulder, SIZ 25	L	T	2d8+1d8+1d6	Bash, Stun Location	10	40	Roll	3m (10 ft)
Boulder, SIZ 50	H	T	3d8+2d10+1d2	Bash, Stun Location	10	60	Roll	1.5m (5 ft)
Boulder, SIZ 75	E	T	4d8+2d10+1d8	Bash, Stun Location	10	80	Roll	1.5m (5 ft)
Pedestal, Stone	S-M	T	1d8	Bash, Stun Location	10	10	Wobble	3m (10 ft)
Stone Statue, Giant-Sized	E	L	2d8+1d8+1d6	Bash, Grip, Stun Location*	10	36	Walk	3m (10 ft)
Stone Statue, Man-Sized	L	M	1d8+1d6	Bash, Grip, Stun Location*	8	18	Walk	4m (15 ft)

* May possess additional Combat Effects if armed

this spell cannot be imbued with INS, and must be commanded to perform any actions throughout the spell's duration. Such commands must be brief - no more than a dozen words.

Astral Spell
(Alteration)

Sphere: Astral

Cost: 1/Intensity

Area: See Below

Casting Time: 30 Minutes

Duration: See Below

Range: Touch

Resist: NA

Other than the changes noted above, this spell functions as per the Arcane spell of the same name.

Confusion
(Enchantment (Charm))

Sphere: Charm

Cost: 3, +1/additional Intensity

Area: 6m (20 ft) Radius

Casting Time: 1 Round

Duration: 3 Rounds/ Intensity

Range: 75m (250 ft)

Resist: Willpower (Hard)

This spell instils a feeling of bewilderment and disorientation in 1d4 creatures, +2 per additional level of Intensity, within the area of effect. Thus, 4 levels of Intensity will affect 1d4+6 creatures; 1d4 for the first Intensity, plus 6 creatures for the additional 3 Intensity. A successful Resistance roll overcomes the spell, while a failed roll results in the victim suffering from one of the following random effects, roll every Round for the spell's duration, or until the victim wanders off.

Each attack on a confused creature allows it an additional attempt to resist the spell. The victim can Evade or Parry normally.

With a 'Wander off' result, the victim heads in the opposite direction to the caster at a walking gait using their normal mode of movement. Creatures with innate abilities such as astral or ethereal travel, plane shifting, etc. have a 50% chance of using one of these abilities in place of their mundane form of movement each round.

Confusion

D100	Effects of Confusion
01-10	Attack the caster with either ranged or melee weapons for the remainder of the round
11-50	Stand confused, essentially choosing Dither for the remainder of the round.
51-70	Attack nearest enemy for the remainder of the round
71-80	Attack nearest ally for the remainder of the round
81-90	Wander off at Walk speed if unengaged for the duration of the spell, otherwise Dither as for 11-50 above
91-00	Act normally for the remainder of the round

Conjure Earth Elemental (Reversible)
(Summoning)

Sphere: Elemental (Earth)

Cost: 3, +1/additional Intensity

Area: See Below

Casting Time: 10 Minutes

Duration: 10 Minutes/Intensity

Range: 36m (120 ft)

New Divine Spells

Resist: NA

Other than the changes noted above, this spell functions as per the Rank 4 spell Conjure Fire Elemental. Use the Fire Elemental Table to determine the specific Earth Elemental summoned.

Control Weather
(Alteration)

Sphere: Weather

Cost: 3, +1/Intensity

Area: 1d4 square miles per Intensity

Casting Time: 10 Minutes

Duration: 1d12 Hours/Intensity

Range: 0

Resist: NA

Other than the changes noted above, this spell functions as per the Arcane spell of the same name.

Earthquake
(Alteration)

Sphere: Elemental (Earth)

Cost: 3, +1/additional Intensity

Area: 3m (10 ft) Radius/Intensity

Casting Time: 10 Minutes

Duration: 1 Minute

Range: 110m (360 ft)

Resist: NA

Once cast, this spell creates a powerful, localised tremor affecting everything in its radius. Each level of Intensity increases the radius by 3 metres (10 feet), and an Athletics roll is required every Round throughout the duration simply to remain standing. The difficulty of all skill rolls is based on the spell's Intensity, except for Endurance and Willpower, which are unaffected. Ground movement is subject to reduction as well at Intensity 3 and higher. These effects are noted on the table opposite.

Creatures and inanimate objects in the area of effect sustain 1d6 damage per Intensity every Round, from falling objects as the tremor destabilizes them, or from tumbling into chasms opened as the earth splits. Common objects are detailed on the Earthquake Susceptibility Table below. After taking sufficient damage, the listed effects should be applied to objects in the area if applicable. The Games Master should refer to the Inanimate Objects Armour and Hit Points Table on page 81 of MYTHRAS and the Common Dungeon Object Table on page 14 for additional objects and their Armour and Hit Points where required.

Many of the effects detailed in the following table feature damage from falling debris. Armour offers only half its normal protective

EARTHQUAKE

Intensity	Radius	Skill Modifier	Move Penalty
1	3m (10 ft)	Standard	-
2	6m (20 ft)	Standard	-
3	9m (30 ft)	Hard	-25%
4	12m (40 ft)	Hard	-25%
5	18m (50 ft)	Formidable	-50%
6	21m (60 ft)	Formidable	-50%
7	24m (70 ft)	Herculean	-75%
8	27m (80 ft)	Herculean	-75%
9	30m (90 ft)	Hopeless	No movement
10	33m (100 ft)	Hopeless	No movement

value with regards to this damage, and as a reminder, it offers no protection from damage resulting from a fall. See table overleaf.

Finger of Death
(Necromancy)

Sphere: Necromantic

Cost: 3/Intensity, +1 EXP

Area: 1 Target

Casting Time: 2 Actions

Duration: Permanent

Range: 18m (60 ft)

Resist: Endurance

While this, the most powerful of death spells, is available to both druids and clerics, typically only evil deities will grant Finger of Death to clerical orders. Clerics of good or neutral morality typically cannot use it. The casting of Finger of Death stops a victim's heart, killing them outright. The victim, which is pointed at throughout the casting, is allowed an Endurance resistance roll. The table below details the Endurance modifier for the victim's Rank or SIZ, whichever gives them the more beneficial result. However, each additional level of Intensity will increase this base difficulty one grade, increasing the likelihood of slaying even the most powerful of adversaries.

FINGER OF DEATH

Target Rank	Target SIZ	Base Endurance Modifier
0-1*	1-20	Formidable
2	21-40	Hard
3	41-60	Standard
4	61-80	Easy
5	81+	Very Easy

* This category includes characters that do not possess a class.

Earthquake Spell - Item Susceptibility

Creature/ Object/Area	Armour Points	Hit Points	Effects
Creature	*	*	Creatures take 1d6 damage to one Body Location per level of Intensity. For example, an Intensity 3 quake would cause 1d6 damage to 3 different locations.
Bridge, Stone	10	40	Every time the bridge's Armour is exceeded, those beneath it that fail to Evade are subjected to a piece of falling debris doing 2d6 damage. When the bridge is reduced to 0 Hit Points, the entire bridge collapses. Those on the bridge at the time suffer falling damage as detailed in MYTHRAS page 78. Any creature that fails an Evade roll while under the bridge takes 2d6 damage to 2 Hit Locations per Intensity of the spell.
Bridge, Wooden	6-8	20	As for Bridge, Stone. However, the damage dice are reduced to 1d10 in each instance.
Cliff	6-10	30	Those unlucky enough to be climbing the cliff during the earthquake are required to make a Climb roll every Round just to remain holding on. If reduced to 0 Hit Points, the entire cliff within the area of effect collapses, causing an avalanche. If this happens, either a Climb or Evade roll is required to determine if the climber is close enough to grab a ledge. Those that fail take falling damage as detailed in MYTHRAS page 78. Being on the ground and near the cliff during the quake requires an Evade roll to avoid falling debris, that fail take 2d6 damage to 2 Hit Locations per Intensity of the spell.
Fountain, Stone	8-10	10-30	When reduced to half Hit Points, the fountain will leak, spilling its contents. However, it will still leave its contents accessible. When reduced to 0 Hit Points the fountain is destroyed, its contents now spilling deep underground.
Stalactite/ Stalagmite	6-8	5-20	Treat as Stone Ceiling and/or Natural Stone Columns, whichever is more appropriate to the actual environment.
Stone Ceiling	10	40**	Every time the ceiling's Armour is exceeded, those within the area of effect that fail to Evade are subjected to a piece of falling debris doing 2d6 damage. When reduced to 0 Hit Points, the entire ceiling within the area of effect comes crashing down. Any creature that fails an Evade roll takes 2d6 damage to 2 Hit Locations per Intensity.
Stone Column, Natural	8-10	10-30	When reduced to 0 Hit Points, the column collapses. Roll on the Missing with a Thrown Weapon Table on page 111 of CLASSIC FANTASY to determine the direction of the collapse. The height of the column determines the area of effect. Any that fail an Evade roll take 2d6 damage to 1d2 random Hit Locations.
Stone Column, Artificial	8-10	10-20	As per Stone Column, Natural
Stone Wall	10	50**	When reduced to 0 Hit Points, half the wall within the area of effect collapses inward. Any creature within 3 metres (10 feet) that fails an Evade roll will take 2d6 damage to 1 Hit Location.
Structure, Stone	8-10	20-100	Treat as Stone Ceiling and/or Stone Walls. However, the damage dice are reduced to 1d10 in each instance.
Structure, Wood	4-6	10-60	Treat as Stone Ceiling and/or Stone Walls. However, the damage dice are reduced to 1d8 in each instance.
Tunnel	6-10	30	As per Stone Ceiling

* As per creature

** Per 1.5m (5 ft) of thickness. Assumes a stone block wall typical of castles and dungeons.

Finger of Death is affective against only living creatures, having no effect on undead, constructs, etc. Victims killed by the spell can be returned to life through the casting of Wish, Raise Dead, Resurrection, and Reincarnation as normal.

Regenerate (Reversible)

(Necromancy)

Sphere: Healing
Cost: 3/Intensity
Area: 1 Creature
Casting Time: 3 Minutes
Duration: Permanent
Range: Touch
Resist: NA (Parry or Evade)

When cast, the cleric regenerates a dismembered body location with a single touch. Lost limbs completely grow back at a rate of 1 Hit Point every 10 minutes until fully healed. However, if the severed location is present and touching the victim, the entire recovery time is reduced to 1 minute. This spell cannot be used to 'clone' an individual by regenerating two separate parts, with only the portion connected to the brain and central nervous system benefiting from the effects of the spell. Each level of Intensity will regrow a separate body location.

When reversed, Wither will cause a location touched by the caster to shrivel up and eventually fall off the victim. The process causes the loss of 1 Hit Point of damage to the impacted location per 10 minutes, with the location becoming unusable at 0 Hit Points, and falling off when fully negative. The effects can only be negated by a casting of Regenerate.

Restoration (Reversible)

(Necromancy)

Sphere: Healing
Cost: 3, +1/additional Intensity
Area: 1 Target
Casting Time: 3 Minutes
Duration: Permanent
Range: Touch
Resist: NA

With the casting of Restoration, a victim previously drained of their life force through the use of Energy Drain or similar effects, regains one previously lost level of Fatigue. At 1 level of Intensity, this spell is only effective on a creature drained within the last 24 hours. Each additional Intensity increases the time that can have passed by a further 24 hours. For example, a victim that was previously drained just under 48 hours ago, would need the spell cast at 2 Intensity to be effective. Multiple levels of drained Fatigue require additional castings of Restoration. Regardless of duration, and in addition to any Fatigue restored, Restoration also restores all other mental effects such as those brought on by the Feeblemind spell, as well as any form of insanity or dementia. This spell is very powerful and draining, costing the caster not only the noted Magic Points, but also aging them 2% of their typical lifespan (2 years in the case of a human caster).

When reversed, Energy Drain imposes one level of Fatigue on the victim with no Resistance Roll possible in the case of an NPC. However, a player character (or any creature or NPC that possesses Luck Points) is allowed a Willpower Resistance roll. Lost Fatigue due to Energy Drain is unaffected by Cure Fatigue spells and potions, and is permanent until cured through the use of a Restoration spell or scroll. Energy Drain does not age the caster or victim in anyway, and is not hindered by armour.

Reincarnation, Divine (Reversible)

(Necromancy)

Sphere: Animal
Cost: 3, +1/additional Intensity, +1 EXP
Area: One Target
Casting Time: 10 Minutes
Duration: Permanent
Range: Touch
Resist: See Below

Other than the changes noted above and in the following text, this spell functions as per the Arcane spell of the same name.

This spell is cast while touching the corpse of a creature dead no longer than one week, however unlike its Arcane counterpart, elves can benefit from Divine Reincarnation.

Roll on the table overleaf to determine the new form.

Reincarnation, Divine

D100	Reincarnation Result
01-15	Human
16-35	Woodland Being
	01-15: Centaur
	16-30: Dryad
	31-45: Faun/Satyr
	46-65: Elf
	66-85: Gnome
	86-00: Pixie
36-85	Woodland Animal
	01-11 Eagle (Animal, Small)
	12-23 Bear
	24-32 Boar
	33-37 Fox (Animal, Small)
	38-46 Hawk (Animal, Small)
	47-53 Lynx (Animal, Small)
	54-60 Owl (Animal, Small)
	61-65 Raccoon (Animal, Small)
	66-76 Stag
	77-88 Wolf
	89-00 Wolverine (Animal, Small)
86-00	Other, GM's Option

Resurrection (Reversible)
(Necromancy)

Sphere: Necromantic

Cost: 3, +1/additional Intensity, +3 EXP

Area: One Target

Casting Time: 10 Minutes

Duration: Permanent

Range: Touch

Resist: NA (Willpower (Formidable))

Resurrection raises any creature, including an elf, dead for no more than 20 years per level of Intensity. The creature is not only given life, but restored to full strength and healed from injury, even restoring lost limbs. Very little of the actual creature needs to remain for the spell to still be effective. For example, Resurrection could be used to bring a being back from the dead after 145 years, even if possessing nothing more than a finger bone, assuming the spell is cast at 8 Intensity. The raised individual requires no period of rest, and is fully functional immediately. The spell has no effect on a creature that died of natural cause at the end of it allotted lifespan.

If the subject's Ethical Passion was anything other than evil, they can resist the spell with an Opposed Willpower Roll and, if successful, negate the effects. This is because the soul or spirit of the deceased is rarely willing to return to the living once it has reached its eternal reward. However, the Games Master can decide to waive the roll if the recipient has unfinished business, cannot be separated from their true love, or has some other heroic reason to live. In the case of evil souls, who would gladly return instead of suffering eternal damnation, it isn't the deceased's Willpower that's resisting, but that of the demon, devil, etc., placed in charge of their punishment, their tormentor. In this case, the caster must overcome the tormentor's Willpower. If this is unknown, assume it is at least 20 points higher than that of the deceased to represent that the stronger the soul's will, the more powerful the being placed in charge of his or her damnation. If the caster succeeds, the subject has been successfully resurrected. While a failed roll results in the victim being either unwilling or unable to return.

Resurrection is very draining, aging the cleric 3% of their typical lifespan (3 years in the case of a human caster).

When reversed, Destruction, can be used to kill one victim in contact with the cleric at the time of the casting. This victim is allowed a Willpower roll to resist, modified by the target's Rank or SIZ, whichever gives the more beneficial result, as detailed on the following table.

If this Resistance roll is unsuccessful, the subject is slain outright, their body being turned to dust. Only the casting of Wish will bring the victim back at this stage. On a successful roll, the subject is still reduced to negative 1d4 Hit Points in the touched body location. Armour offers no protection from this damage. Destruction does not age the caster when used.

Resurrection

Target Rank	Target SIZ	Willpower Modifier
0-1*	1-20	Formidable
2	21-40	Hard
3	41-60	Standard
4	61-80	Easy
5	81+	Very Easy

* This category includes characters that do not possess a class.

Mind Slayers

Mind Slayers resemble slimy, human-size humanoids with octopus-like heads, and large, dead, white eyes. Four long tentacles hang from the bottom of the creature's face covering a round, lamprey-like mouth, and each hand possesses three long boney fingers and a thumb. Mind slayers feed on the brains of all other creatures that cross their path, hating most living things. They keep captives as both slaves and food, often seeking enjoyment in their torment and pain. Captives showing promise are often used in gladiatorial sport; others are treated as nothing more than cattle. They are both amphibious and capable swimmers. Mind slayers possess a strong dislike for sunlight, preferring to live a subterranean existence. They can speak, and know their own racial language as well as that of many of the sapient denizens of the Underdeep, but prefer the use of telepathy. Mind slayers are hermaphroditic, each able to produce one young "tadpole" twice in their lifetime.

Mind slayers are psychic creatures, possessing several different powers of the mind with which they attack and/or manipulate their victims. Each is born with Telepathy, and learn Mind Blast as their first trained psychic ability. Both of these abilities are not typically able to be learned until higher levels of skill is obtained in other psychic creatures or individuals. An average mind slayer knows the psychic disciplines noted in its stat block taking into account the Psychic Manipulation and Willpower skill levels noted. See Psychic Abilities on page 26 for an overview on the use of these powers. Mind slayers are not averse to leaving both their treasure and their allies and fleeing combat if things are going against them, and will never willingly fight to the death.

To feed, a mind slayer typically uses its power of Domination to put their prey into a deep trance. Once pacified, the creature's long tentacles wrap around the victim's head and penetrate the skull, reaching the brain in 1d3+1 rounds. The brain is then drawn from the victim, killing them instantly and devoured by the creature for psychic nourishment.

Mind slayers are seldom encountered in any but the deepest of dungeons and caverns. Their species originates from the depths of the Underdeep, in the deepest and darkest confines of the earth. They are rumored to live in vast subterranean cities like the dark elves, with which they are the fiercest of rivals.

Mind Slayer		Attributes	
STR: 3d6 (11)		Action Points	4 (multi-limbed)
CON: 3d6+6 (17)		Damage Modifier	None
SIZ: 2d6+6 (13)		Magic Points	19
DEX: 2d6+9 (16)		Movement	6m (20')
INT: 1d6+14 (18)		Initiative Bonus	17
POW: 2d6+12 (19)		No. Appearing	1d4 (10d10x20)
CHA: 2d6 (7)		Treasure Type	(D, E, F, M)

1d20	Location	AP/HP
1–3	Right Leg	0/6
4–6	Left Leg	0/6
7–9	Abdomen	0/7
10-12	Chest	0/8
13–15	Right Arm	0/5
16–18	Left Arm	0/5
19–20	Head	0/6

Passions

Lawful (Prideful and Selfish) 67%, Evil (Cannibalistic, Enjoys Harming Oppressing and Killing Others, and Hates Good) 67%

Skills

Athletics 47%, Brawn 44%, Customs 76%, Deceit 55%, Endurance 64%, Evade 62%, Insight 77%, Languages (Mind Slayer, Dark Elf, and Underdeep) 65%, Locale 76%, Perception 77%, Psychic Manipulation 78%, Stealth 62%, Willpower 78%

Psychic Disciplines

Astral Projection, Body Equilibrium, Domination, ESP, Levitation, Mind Blast, Probability Travel, and Telepathy. The mind slayer's Telepathy has evolved as its normal mode of communication, and therefore has no cost in Fatigue. Mind blast is unique to the mind slayer and detailed in its description.

Combat Style & Weapons

Tentacle Terror (Claws, Tentacles) 67%

Weapon	Size/Force	Reach	Damage	AP/HP
Claws	M	M	1d4	As for Arm
Tentacles	M	M	None*	As for Head

* Mind slayers typically attempt to score a Grip Special Effect when attacking with their tentacles.

Psychic Powers

Some CLASSIC FANTASY monsters possess psychic powers. These abilities, while apparently magic to most observers, do not detect or dispel as would an arcane or divine spell. They are powers of the mind, and difficult to contend with by the unprepared. Psychic Powers are detailed here as they are the primary abilities of the Mind Slayer, as well as other monsters to be included in future CLASSIC FANTASY products. This is not to say that they cannot be used by player characters; but be aware that psychic powers bring a different energy to the game and may need careful consideration to avoid disrupting an existing campaign. Game Masters are free to allow their use by one or more player characters as they see fit. And indeed, Psychic Powers have played a part in even the earliest of level based fantasy games. Psychic powers should be rare though, with no more than one-percent of adventurers possessing Psychic Powers.

Psychic Practitioners

The manipulation of psychic powers, hereafter called *disciplines*, requires one core skill: Psychic Manipulation. Psychic Manipulation is the skill of manipulating psychic disciplines. While Psychic Manipulation is defined as a Professional skill, it cannot be learned in the same way as other Professional skills, being possessed by only a few gifted individuals or, in some cases, entire species. Most, if not all, offensive disciplines are opposed by the Willpower of the victim. Willpower reflects the user's mental strength with regards to overcoming mental and psychic trauma. Willpower is of course possessed by all sapient creatures.

Psychic Manipulation (POWx2)

Psychic Manipulation represents a psychic's ability to successfully use psychic disciplines. Unlike spells, most psychic disciplines do not use Intensity in calculating their effects. For those that do, figure Intensity as equal to one tenth the user's Psychic Manipulation skill. Psychic disciplines are not magic and cannot be dispelled, therefore they have no need of a Magnitude.

Psychic Practitioners and Rank

Unlike arcane and divine spells, psychic disciplines are not categorised by Rank. Disciplines fall into either Minor or Major categories. A Minor discipline can be used by any practitioner as long as they possess the Psychic Manipulation skill. Major disciplines require the practitioner to possess both Psychic Manipulation and Willpower scores of at least 70%.

Psychic Disciplines Known

Psychic entities know a number of psychic disciplines equal to 1/10th their Psychic Manipulation skill. If the Game Master is closely tracking such information with regards to a non-player character, it requires the expenditure of an Experience Roll to acquire a new psychic discipline assuming Psychic Manipulation has been raised to a sufficient level. The practitioner typically knows only Minor disciplines until 70%, after which they can learn either Minor or Major disciplines as desired. Psychic disciplines do not require prior memorization; all known psychic disciplines can be used as needed.

Use Requirements

A psychic practitioner does require the ability to accurately perceive or sense a potential target, if the discipline has to be targeted. Psychic disciplines do not require verbal or material components in their use. However, while somatic gestures are not required, if the user isn't able to touch their forehead, or hold an outstretched arm, tentacle, etc. in the direction of a potential target to aid in focusing their concentration, the Psychic Manipulation skill becomes one grade harder.

All psychic disciplines require two Actions, the first spent in concentration. The next Action is when the discipline takes effect.

Restricted Actions

A psychic practitioner is subject to the same limitations placed upon spell casters with regards to allowed actions. See Restricted Actions During Casting on page 121 of CLASSIC FANTASY.

Interrupting Use

A psychic practitioner is subject to the same limitations placed upon spell casters with regards to having their discipline disrupted. See Interrupting Casting on page 121 of CLASSIC FANTASY.

Armor and Psychic Practitioners

The use of psychic disciplines is not affected by armor in any way.

Psychic Discipline Cost

Psychic disciplines are not magic and therefore do not require the expenditure of magic points in their use. But hey are mentally exhausting, and this requires the user to expend levels of fatigue for continued use. The first use of a psychic discipline in a Scene is always at no loss of Fatigue; each psychic discipline used after the first requires a Willpower roll, with each roll at a cumulative one grade of difficulty. Failure results in the loss of one level of Fatigue.

Dismissing a Psychic Discipline

A psychic practitioner can dismiss any psychic discipline they have invoked as a Free Action. No roll is needed; simply the cessation of the effects.

Stacking Psychic Disciplines

Psychic disciplines cannot be stacked with magic spells to produce greater effects. In addition, multiple psychic disciplines which have a similar purpose cannot be stacked. In situations where two incompatible psychic disciplines/spells are in simultaneous existence, the discipline or magic with the greater Intensity take precedence, suppressing or subsuming the lesser power. Where both are of equal Intensity, the newer replaces the previous. In cases where both offer differing effects, they both exist simultaneously.

Psychic Disciplines and Range

All psychic disciplines have a range of 1.5 metres (5 feet) times the practitioner's Willpower unless noted otherwise, with the exception of psychic disciplines that affect the practitioner only.

Psychic Disciplines and Damage

Psychic disciplines that cause damage do so as per spells unless noted otherwise. See Spell Damage on page 124 of CLASSIC FANTASY.

Resisting a Psychic Discipline

Targets of a psychic discipline can resist the effects inan Opposed roll of Willpower vs the Psychic Manipulation skill of the practitioner.

Psychic Disciplines

Astral Projection (Major)

By means of this discipline, a practitioner is able to leave their physical body and enter the Astral Plane. This discipline has a duration lasting as long as long as the practitioner wishes, or until terminated by some outside force, such the death of the practitioner's physical body. This discipline functions in all ways as per the cleric's Astral Spell. See Chapter 14 of CLASSIC FANTASY for additional information on the Astral Plane.

Body Equilibrium (Minor)

This psychic discipline enables the practitioner to alter their weight enough to walk across any surface without so much as leaving an imprint for as long as they maintain concentration. This goes so far as to even include water, mud, quicksand, and so on. Treat as per the spell Feather Fall with regards to falling.

Domination (Minor)

This psychic discipline is used to bend the will of one individual within range. The victim is allowed an Opposed Willpower roll to resist; if the resistance fails, the target is mentally under the control of the psychic. If they are forced to do something obviously harmful or dangerous, or forced to do something contrary to one of their Passions, they are immediately allowed a further resistance roll to break free, with the resistance being one grade easier.

ESP (Minor)

This psychic discipline allows the practitioner to read the surface thoughts of any being within range. Undead, and those with minds alien to the practitioner, tend toi be unreadable, or simply a psychic representation of white noise. The amount of information gained from the reading depends on the level of intelligence possessed by the target. For example, a sapient being can have quite detailed and specific thoughts, while a non-sapient animal might just be thinking about food, mating, and so on. Unlike the spell of the same name, the practitioner is required to know the language that the subject "thinks" in with regards to detailed information. Where multiple languages are known, assume the subject thinks in their native/racial tongue. In situations where the subject's language is not known by the practitioner, only psychic white noise is perceived.

Levitation (Minor)

This psychic discipline enables the practitioner to float either straight up or down for as long as they maintain concentration. Horizontal movement is not granted. The maximum that can be lifted is the practitioner themselves and no more than 10 additional Encumbrance. The maximum height that can be reached is equal to the practitioner's Psychic Manipulation percentage in metres (or 3 times the percentage in feet).

Mind Blast (Major)

This psychic discipline is an innate ability possessed by the Mind Slayer and the first ability they are trained in (they are born with Telepathy). It is therefore treated as a Minor Discipline with regards to their development. Mind Blast is the primary offensive ability used by the Mind Slayer in combat and is a blast of pure psychic energy. It is concentrated in the direction the slayer is facing to a range of 18 Metres (60 feet), and expands in a cone shaped area of effect 6 metres (20 feet) wide at the extreme end of the blast. All those caught in the blast must make an opposed roll of Willpower vs. the Psychic Manipulation skill roll. If the defender fails, then they are rendered insensible for 3d4 Rounds. When hunting for slaves or food, a mind slayer typically uses Mind Blast to incapacitate a victim before carrying them off to whatever terrible fate it has planned for the wretch.

Probability Travel (Major)

This psychic discipline allows the practitioner and one or more companions to travel to planes beyond the Prime Material. This includes the Ethereal Plane, and those planes only reachable by travelling through the Ethereal. Additional individuals can accompany the practitioner, with every two companions (rounded up) increasing the difficulty of the Psychic Manipulation roll by one grade. Probability Travel offers more options than Astral Projection, although the user must expend one level of Fatigue after each use, including the first. This first roll requires no Willpower roll. On a failed Psychic Manipulation roll, the practitioner and all companions become lost, ending up in location determined by the Games Master.

Telepathy (Major)

This psychic discipline is an innate ability possessed by the Mind Slayer, and is therefore treated as a Minor Discipline with regards to their development. Telepathy places the practitioner in mind-to-mind contact with another sapient being, allowing for normal levels of communication. Telepathy eliminates the requirement that the practitioner know the language spoken by the subject. The target of Telepathy must be within line-of-sight (range is of no consequence) unless well-known by the practitioner. If the practitioner knows the subject well, contact can be established as long as both the subject and practitioner occupy the same plane of existence and are within a distance of no greater than 300,000 kilometres (186,000 miles/1 light second); line-of-sight is obviously irrelevant.

Updated Tables

Level 6 and Level 7 Dungeon Encounter Table

Level 6	Level 7	Encounter (On level 7 increase chance of a leader by 10% and a spell caster by 5%)
01-10	01-10	Roll on the Level 4-5 Table
11-50	11-45	Common
		01-20: 1d8+3 Orcs. 70% chance of one being a leader and 25% chance of one being a spell caster
		21-35: 1d4+2 Orcs plus 1d3 Ogre subordinates. 70% chance of one orc being a leader.
		36-55: 1d8+1 Gnolls. 60% chance of one being a leader and 20% chance of one being a spell caster
		56-70: 1d8+1 Troglodytes. 60% chance of one being a leader and 20% chance of one being a spell caster
		71-80: 1d3+1 Hill Giants. 20% chance of one being a leader
		81-85: 1d2 Hill Giants plus 1d2 Ogre subordinates. No more than 8 Ogres total will be found accompanying Fire Giants on any given dungeon level
		86-90: 1d2 Hill Giants plus 1d3 Giant Lizards. No more than 3 Giant Lizards total will be found accompanying Hill Giants on any given dungeon level
		91-00: 1d2 Hill Giants plus 1d3+1 Dire Wolves. No more than 16 Dire Wolves total will be found accompanying Hill Giants on any given dungeon level
51-75	46-65	Uncommon
		01-20: 1d8+3 Hobgoblins. 70% chance of one being a leader and 25% chance of one being a spell caster
		21-35: 1d2 Hobgoblins plus 1d6+2 Goblin subordinates. 70% chance of one hobgoblin being a leader
		36-45: 1d2 Hobgoblins plus 1d4+2 Orc subordinates. 70% chance of one hobgoblin being a leader
		46-55: 1d6+2 Bugbears. 60% chance of one being a leader and 20% chance of one being a spell caster
		56-65: 1d8+1 Lizard Men. 60% chance of one being a leader and 20% chance of one being a spell caster
		66-70: 1d4+2 Ogres
		71-75: 1 Basilisk
		76-80: 1d2+1 Stone Giants
		81-85: 1d2 Stone Giants plus 1 Cave Bear (also known as a Short-Faced Bear, See Bear)
		86-90: 1 Mimic (10% chance of a killer mimic)
		91-95: 1d3 Trolls
		96-00: 2d6+1 patches of Green Slime 1.5 metres (5 feet) in size (these can be linked together forming larger patches, or spread around as numerous small patches, as decided by the Games Master)
76-85	66-80	Rare
		01-05: 1 Black Dragon; 01-75 young adult, 76-00 adult
		06-07: 1 Brass Dragon; 01-75 young adult, 76-00 adult
		08-15: 1 White Dragon; 01-75 young adult, 76-00 adult
		16-19: 1 Gorgon, Greater (see Gorgon in MYTHRAS)
		20-24: 1d2 Wyverns
		25-31: 1d2 Ettins
		32-36: 1d2 Fire Giants

Level 6 and Level 7 Dungeon Encounter Table

Level 6	Level 7	Encounter (On level 7 increase chance of a leader by 10% and a spell caster by 5%)
		37-41: 1 Fire Giant plus 1d4 Hell Hounds (large: STR+3 and SIZ+6). No more than 4 Hell Hounds total will be found accompanying Fire Giants on any given dungeon level
		42-46: 1d2 Frost Giants
		47-50: 1 Frost Giant plus 1d2 Winter Wolves. Treat as white Dire Wolves that breathe a blast of cold. This cold functions as does the breath of the Hell Hound with regards to range, area, and damage, however will obviously not set fires. No more than 6 Winter Wolves total will be found among Frost Giants on any given dungeon level
		51-54: 1 Mind Slayer
		55-61: 1d2+1 Rust Monsters
		62-66: 1d6+6 patches of Brown Mould 1.5 metres (5 feet) in size (these can be linked together forming larger patches, or spread around as numerous small patches, as decided by the Games Master)
		67-71: 1 Chimera
		72-76: 1 Mummy
		77-80: 1 Spirit Naga
		81-85: 1 Giant Scorpion
		86-91: 1 Lurker
		92-00: 1 Carrion Creeper
86-90	81-90	Very Rare
		01-05: 1 Blue Dragon; 01-75 juvenile, 76-00 young adult
		06-07: 1 Bronze Dragon; 01-75 juvenile, 76-00 young adult
		08-09: 1 Copper Dragon; 01-75 young adult, 76-00 adult
		10-11: 1 Gold Dragon; 01-75 juvenile, 76-00 young adult
		12-16: 1 Green Dragon; 01-75 young adult, 76-00 adult
		17-21: 1 Red Dragon; 01-75 juvenile, 76-00 young adult
		22-23: 1 Silver Dragon; 01-75 juvenile, 76-00 young adult
		24-30: Elemental of 1d6+6 SIZ (01-25 Earth, 26-50 Air, 51-75 Fire. 76-00 Water) They are typically found in or around examples of their parent element.
		31-40: 1 Mimic (10% chance of a killer mimic)
		41-50: 1d2 Werebears (see Lycanthropes)
		51-70: Dark Elf War Party (typically 1d6+6 Rank 1 dark elf warriors as per the Dark Elf write-up. However, in a party composed of males, one will be a Rank 1 fighter/magic-user and another a Rank 2 fighter. While in a party of females one will be a Rank 1 cleric and another a Rank 2 fighter.
		71-80: 1d3 Rank 2 and 1d3 Rank 3 Adventurers
		81-90: 1d4 Rank 2 and 1d4 Rank 3 Dwarves (typically dwarf warriors as per Dwarf write-up, however there is a 50% chance that one of the Rank 3 will be serving as their leader
		91-92: 1d4 Rank 2 and 1d4 Rank 3 Elves (typically elf warriors as per Elf write-up, however there is a 50% chance that one of the Rank 3 will be serving as their leader
		93-00: 1d4 Rank 2 and 1d4 Rank 3 Gnomes (typically gnome warriors as per gnome write-up, however there is a 50% chance that one of the Rank 3 will be serving as their leader
91-00	91-00	Roll once again on this table, adding +10% to determine rarity, and treating a further roll of 91-00 as Very Rare. In addition, increase the chance of a leader being present by 10% and where relevant, a spell caster by 5%.

Master Spell List: Arcane, Rank 4

D100 Roll	Spell	School
01-10	Control Weather	Alteration
11-20	Death Spell	Necromancy
21-30	Fireball, Delayed Blast	Evocation
31-40	Flesh to Stone	Alteration
41-50	Globe of Invulnerability	Abjuration
51-60	Invisible Stalker	Summoning
61-70	Monster Summoning, Greater	Summoning
71-80	Reincarnation, Arcane	Necromancy
81-90	True Seeing	Divination
91-00	Word of Power - Blind	Summoning

Master Spell List: Arcane, Rank 5

D100 Roll	Spell	School
01-15	Astral Spell	Alteration
16-30	Mass Charm	Enchantment (Charm)
31-50	Meteor Shower	Evocation
51-70	Monster Summoning, Ultimate	Summoning
71-85	Word of Power - Kill	Summoning
86-00	Time Stop	Alteration
61-70	Monster Summoning, Greater	Summoning
71-80	Reincarnation, Arcane	Necromancy
81-90	True Seeing	Divination
91-00	Word of Power - Blind	Summoning

Master Spell List: Divine Spells, Rank 4

Cleric D100	Druid D100	Spell	Cleric (Pantheonic)	Druid	School	Sphere
-	01-10	Animal Growth	-	Major	Alteration	Animal
-	11-25	Animal Summoning II	-	Major	Conjuration	Animal
01-05	-	Animate Object	Major	-	Alteration	Creation, Summoning
06-15	26-35	Commune	Major	Minor	Divination	Divination
-	36-45	Control Winds	-	Major	Alteration	Weather
16-20	46-55	Conjure Fire Elemental*	Minor	Major	Summoning	Elemental (Fire)
21-30	-	Dispel Evil	Major	-	Abjuration	Protection, Summoning
31-35	-	Flame Strike	Major	-	Evocation	Combat
36-45	56-65	Heal	Major	Major	Necromancy	Healing
46-55	66-70	Insect Plague	Major	-	Summoning	Animal, Combat
56-60	71-80	Part Water	Minor	Major	Alteration	Elemental (Water)
61-65	-	Plane Shift	Major	-	Alteration	Astral
66-75	-	Raise Dead	Major	-	Necromancy	Necromantic
75-85	81-90	Rock to Mud	Minor	Major	Alteration	Elemental (Earth, Water)
86-95	91-00	True Seeing	Major	Minor	Divination	Divination
96-00	-	Weather Summoning	Major	-	Summoning	Summoning

Master Spell List: Divine Spells, Rank 5

Cleric D100	Druid D100	Spell	Cleric (Pantheonic)	Druid	School	Sphere
01-10	-	Animate Rock	Minor	-	Alteration	Elemental (Earth)
11-20	-	Astral Spell	Major	-	Alteration	Astral
21-30	-	Confusion	Major	-	Enchantment (Charm)	Charm
31-45	-	Conjure Earth Elemental	Minor	-	Summoning	Elemental (Earth)
-	01-25	Control Weather	-	Major	Alteration	Weather
46-55	-	Earthquake	Minor	-	Alteration	Elemental (Earth)
56-65	-	Finger of Death	Major	-	Necromancy	Necromantic
66-80	26-50	Regenerate	Major	Major	Necromancy	Healing
81-90	51-75	Restoration	Major	Major	Necromancy	Healing
-	76-00	Reincarnation, Divine	-	Major	Necromancy	Animal
91-00	-	Resurrection	Major	-	Necromancy	Necromantic